PIANO / VOCAL / GUITAR

CHART HITS OF 2018-2019

ISBN 978-1-5400-4718-2

Hal•Leonard®

Visit Hal Leonard Online at
www.halleonard.com

Contact us:
Hal Leonard
7777 West Bluemound Road
Milwaukee, WI 53213
Email: info@halleonard.com

In Europe, contact:
Hal Leonard Europe Limited
42 Wigmore Street
Marylebone, London, W1U 2RN
Email: info@halleonardeurope.com

In Australia, contact:
Hal Leonard Australia Pty. Ltd.
4 Lentara Court
Cheltenham, Victoria, 3192 Australia
Email: info@halleonard.com.au

BETTER NOW

Words and Music by AUSTIN POST
CARL ROSEN, ADAM FEENEY
LOUIS BELL, WILLIAM WALSH
and KAAN GUNESBERK

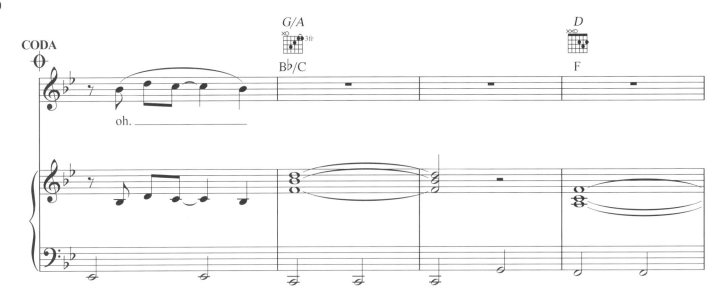

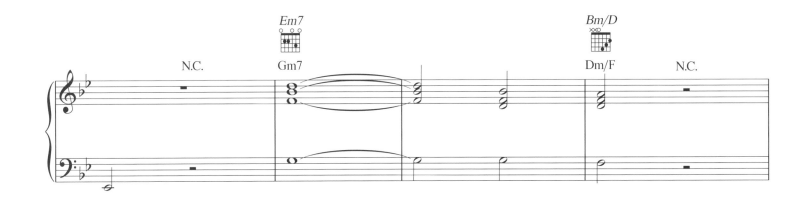

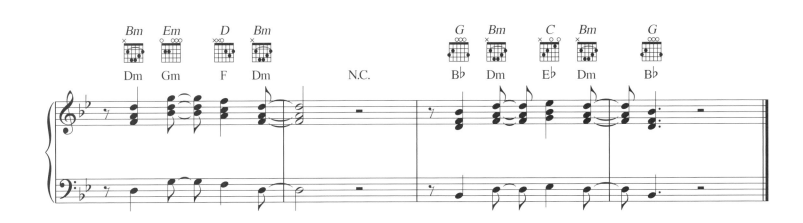

BREATHIN

Words and Music by ARIANA GRANDE,
SAVAN KOTECHA, MAX MARTIN and ILYA

and breath - ing. _____ I know __ I've got to keep, keep __ on breath -

- ing. Mmm. _____ Some - times it's

hard __ to find, _____ find my way __ up in - to the clouds,

tune it out, __ they can be so loud. You re - mind _____

EASTSIDE

Words and Music by BENJAMIN LEVIN,
NATHAN PEREZ, ASHLEY FRANGIPANE,
ED SHEERAN and KHALID ROBINSON

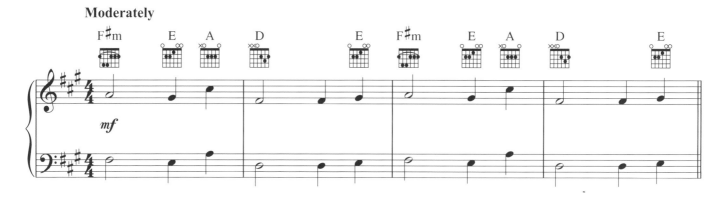

Male: When I was young, I fell in love. We used ___ to hold hands, man, that was e-nough.

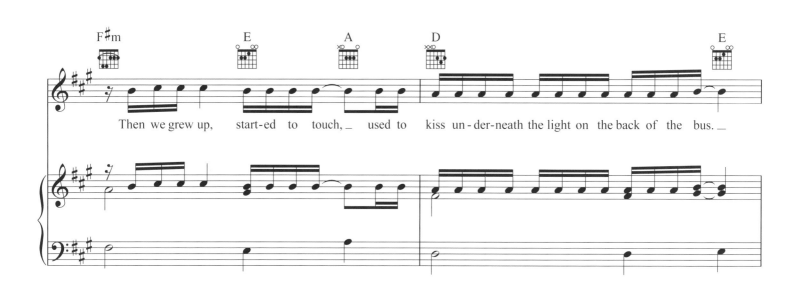

Then we grew up, start-ed to touch, ___ used to kiss un-der-neath the light on the back of the bus. ___

Female vocal written an octave higher than sung.

HAPPIER

Words and Music by MARSHMELLO,
STEVE MAC and DAN SMITH

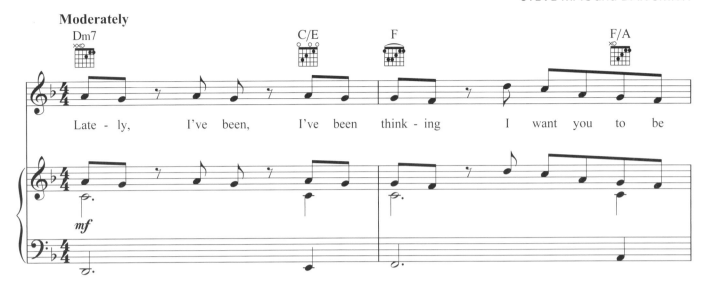

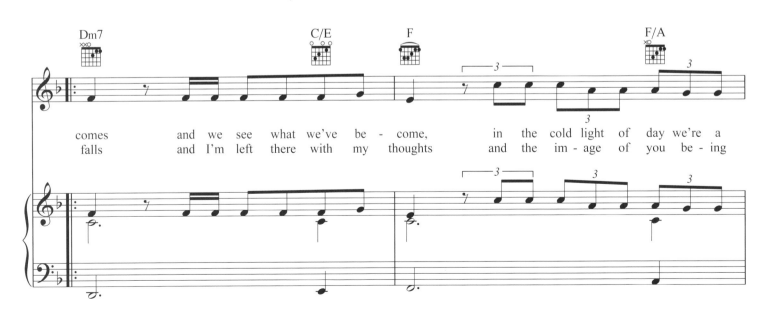

HIGH HOPES

Words and Music by BRENDON URIE,
SAMUEL HOLLANDER, WILLIAM LOBBAN BEAN,
JONAS JEBERG, JACOB SINCLAIR,
JENNY OWEN YOUNGS, ILSEY JUBER,
LAUREN PRITCHARD and TAYLOR PARKS

high, high hopes. _____ Had to have high, high hopes for a

liv - ing. Did - n't know how, but I al - ways had a feel - ing I was gon - na

be that one in a mil - lion. Al - ways had high, high hopes. _____

D.S. al Coda

CODA Am

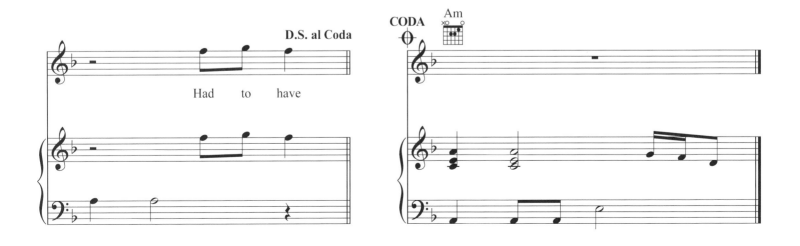

Had to have

BROKEN

Words and Music by MITCHELL COLLINS,
CHRISTIAN MEDICE and SAMANTHA DeROSA

LOVE LIES

Words and Music by KHALID ROBINSON,
NORMANI KORDEI HAMILTON, TAYLA PARX,
JAMIL GEORGE CHAMMAS and RYAN VOJTESAK

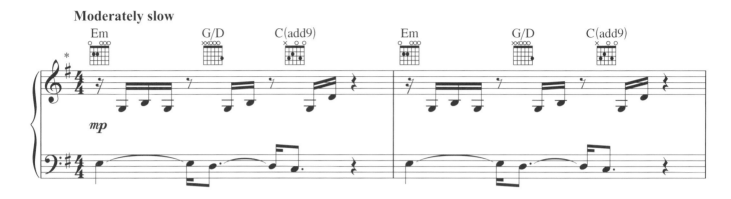

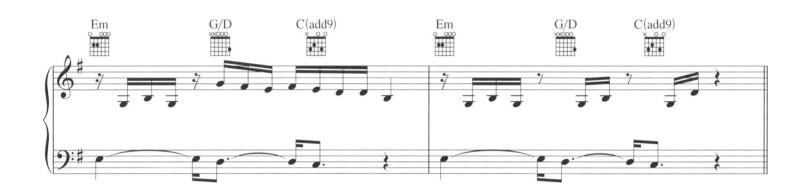

Male: Sor - ry if it's hard to catch my vibe. Mmm, I need a

* *Recorded a half step lower.*

LOVE SOMEONE

Words and Music by LUKAS FORCHHAMMER,
MORTEN RISTORP, MORTEN PILEGAARD,
JARAMYE DANIELS, DON STEFANO,
DAVID LaBREL and JAMES GHALEB

LUCID DREAMS

Words and Music by JARAD HIGGINS,
DOMINIC MILLER, GORDON SUMNER,
DANNY SNODGRASS JR. and NICHOLAS MIRA

NATURAL

Words and Music by DAN REYNOLDS,
WAYNE SERMON, BEN McKEE,
DANIEL PLATZMAN, JUSTIN TRANTOR,
MATTIAS LARSSON and ROBIN FREDRICKSSON

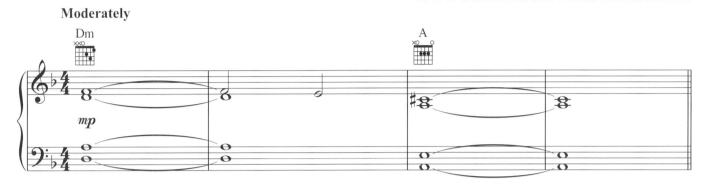

Well, you hold ___ the line ___ when ev-'ry one of them is giv-ing up and giv-ing in, tell me.

In this house ___ of mine, ___ noth-ing ev-er comes with-out a con-se-quence or cost, tell me.

NOTHING BREAKS LIKE A HEART

Words and Music by MARK RONSON,
MILEY CYRUS, THOMAS BRENNECK,
CONOR SZYMANSKI, ILSEY JUBER,
MAXIME PICARD and CLEMENT PICARD

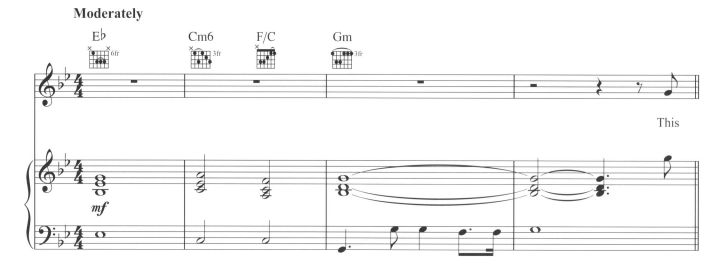

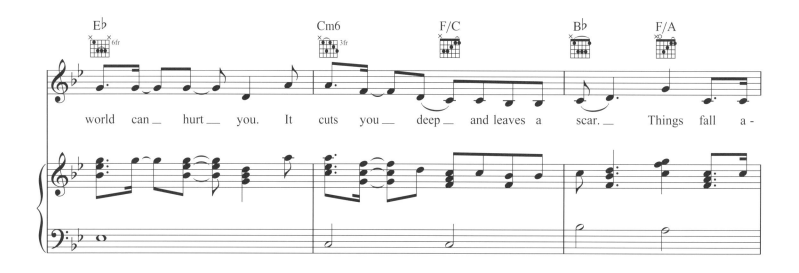

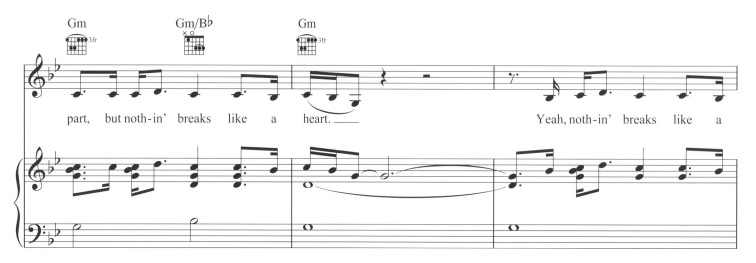

SHALLOW
from A STAR IS BORN

Words and Music by STEFANI GERMANOTTA,
MARK RONSON, ANDREW WYATT
and ANTHONY ROSSOMANDO

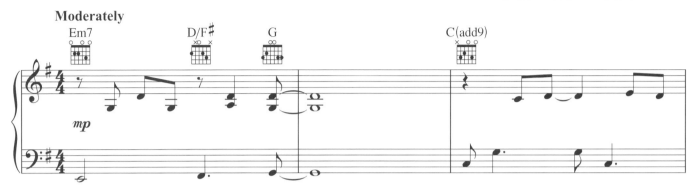

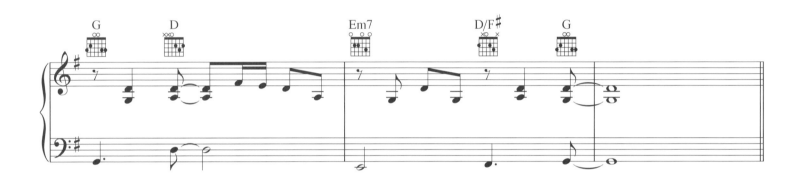

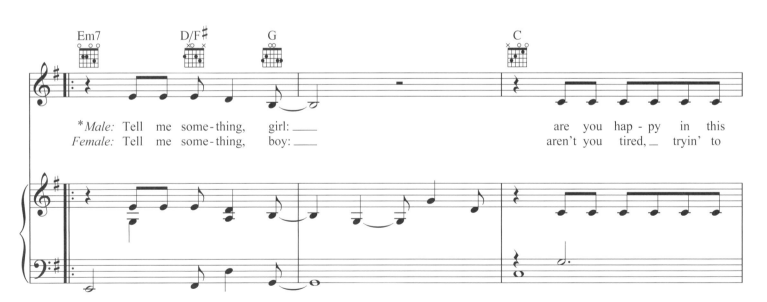

* *Male vocal written at sung pitch.*

THANK U, NEXT

Words and Music by ARIANA GRANDE,
VICTORIA McCANTS, KIMBERLY KRYSIUK,
TAYLOR PARKS, TOMMY BROWN,
CHARLES ANDERSON and MICHAEL FOSTER

Moderate R&B groove

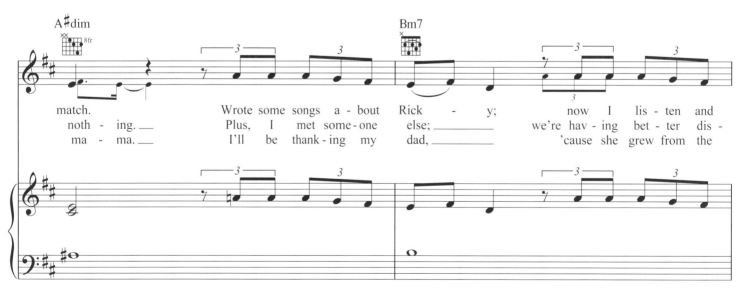

* *Recorded a half step lower.*

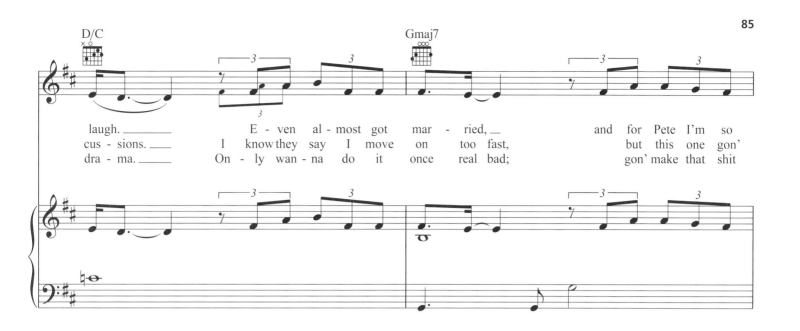

laugh. _____ E - ven al - most got mar - ried, ___ and for Pete I'm so
cus - sions. ____ I know they say I move on too fast, ___ but this one gon'
dra - ma. ____ On - ly wan - na do it once real bad; ___ gon' make that shit

thank - ful. Wish I could say "thank you" to Mal - colm, ___ 'cause he was an
last, _____ 'cause her name is Ar - i, ____ and I'm so good with
last. _____ God for - bid some - thing hap - pens. ___ 'Least this song is a

an - gel. ___ One taught _ me love, one taught _ me
that. _____ She taught _ me love, she taught _ me
smash. _____ I've got so ___ much love, got so ___ much

TRIP

Words and Music by ELLA MAI HOWELL,
DIJON McFARLANE, VARREN JEROME LLOYD WADE
and QUINTON COOK

WITHOUT ME

Words and Music by ASHLEY FRANGIPANE,
BRITTANY AMARADIO, CARL ROSEN,
JUSTIN TIMBERLAKE, SCOTT STORCH,
LOUIS BELL, AMY ALLEN
and TIMOTHY MOSLEY

Slow R&B groove

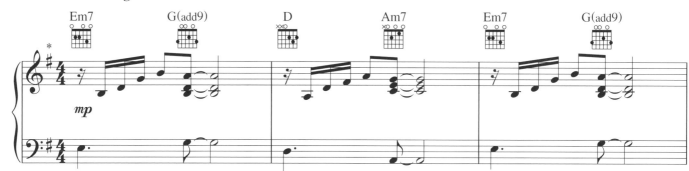

Found you when your heart was broke.
Gave love 'bout a hun-dred tries.

I filled your cup un-til it o-ver-flowed. Took it so far to keep you close.
Just run-ning from the de-mons in your mind. Then I took yours and made them mine.

* *Recorded a half step lower.*

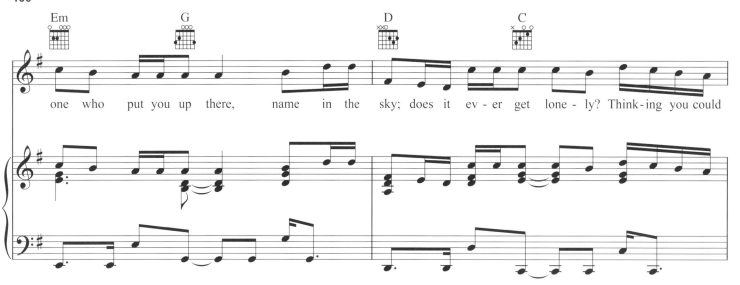

one who put you up there, name in the sky; does it ev-er get lone-ly? Think-ing you could

live _____ with-out _ me. _ Think-ing you could live _____ with-out _ me. Ba-by, I'm the

one who put you up there. I don't know why. (Yeah, I don't know why.)

SUNFLOWER

from SPIDER-MAN: INTO THE SPIDER-VERSE

Words and Music by AUSTIN RICHARD POST,
LOUIS BELL, SWAE LEE,
BILLY WALSH, CARL ROSEN,
CARTER LANG and KHALIF BROWN

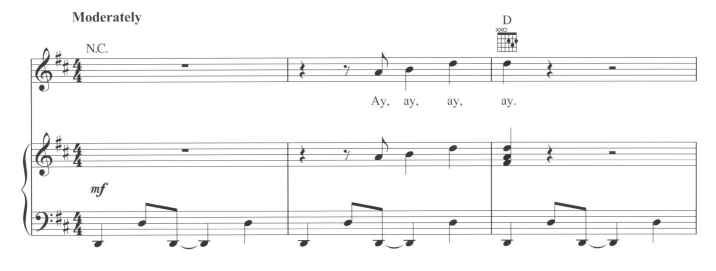

YOU SAY

Words and Music by LAUREN DAIGLE,
JASON INGRAM and PAUL MABURY

Moderately

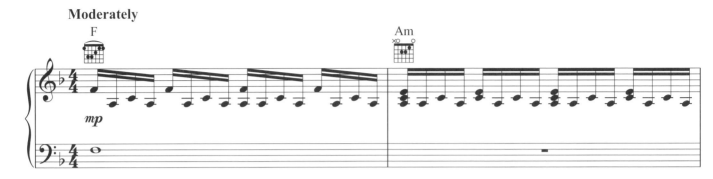

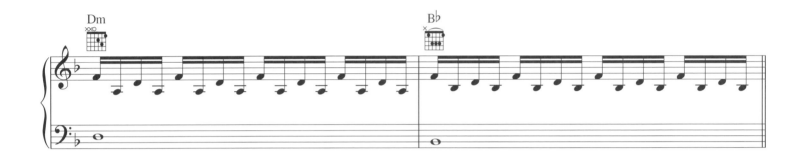

I keep fight-ing voic-es in my mind that say I'm not e-nough,

Oh, I be - lieve. ___ Yes, I be - lieve ___

___ what You say ___ of me. ___ I be - lieve. ___

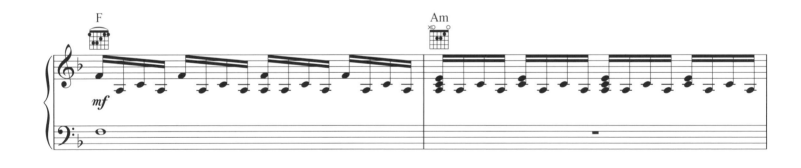

YOUNGBLOOD

Words and Music by ASHTON IRWIN,
CALUM HOOD, LOUIS BELL,
LUKE HEMMING, ALEXANDRA TAMPOSI
and ANDREW WATT